Potty Talk

103 Things To Say When You Leave The Bathroom

By

Aaron Forrester

103 Things To Say When You Leave The Bathroom

Elk Mountain Books
PO Box 21
Wilsonville, Oregon 97070

Potty Talk
103 Things To Say When You Leave The Bathroom

103 Things To Say When You Leave The Bathroom

A Humor Collection

ISBN: 1450577865

Elk Mountain Books titles are available for special promotions and premiums.
For details contact: sales@elkmountainbooks.com

103 Things To Say When You Leave The Bathroom

Aaron Forrester grew up in the Pacific Northwest with a father and four brothers. He currently resides in southwest Virginia with two boys of his own and a loving, patient wife.

103 Things To Say When You Leave The Bathroom

"The idea for the book came from being at parties in college and after graduation when people would return from the bathroom and say the same old line every time, 'I think something died in there!'

So, I decided to take it upon myself to expand the arsenal for those small-time party comics. Everyone laughed but my mom."

~ Aaron

103 Things To Say When You Leave The Bathroom

103 Things To Say When You Leave The Bathroom

1. Dude, I think I plugged your ceiling fan.

103 Things To Say When You Leave The Bathroom

2.   If you were planning to remodel, I just put you ahead of the game.

103 Things To Say When You Leave The Bathroom

3.   Was your wallpaper always peeling like that?

103 Things To Say When You Leave The Bathroom

4.   Anyone have a coat hanger, or a long pointy stick?

103 Things To Say When You Leave The Bathroom

5.   You may want to call an exorcist.

103 Things To Say When You Leave The Bathroom

6.   I would lock that door and not go in there. Ever.

103 Things To Say When You Leave The Bathroom

7.   I think I actually passed out for a minute.

8.   Is it normal to feel all weak and shaky?

103 Things To Say When You Leave The Bathroom

9.   I am so sorry for what I just did.

103 Things To Say When You Leave The Bathroom

10. Okay...so...childbirth isn't so bad!

103 Things To Say When You Leave The Bathroom

11. I think your walls actually gagged.

12. Whoa, that thing looks like a manatee!

103 Things To Say When You Leave The Bathroom

13. I just made brownies if anyone wants some.

103 Things To Say When You Leave The Bathroom

14. Do you have any crime scene tape?

103 Things To Say When You Leave The Bathroom

15. Do you have a bigger plunger?

103 Things To Say When You Leave The Bathroom

16. My eyes are burning! My eyes are burning!

103 Things To Say When You Leave The Bathroom

17. Can someone go ahead and dial 911?

18. You should really put something in there to brace yourself with!

103 Things To Say When You Leave The Bathroom

19. If your kids start crying, I apologize.

20. Um...your cat is trying to bury your toilet.

103 Things To Say When You Leave The Bathroom

21. Do you have a plastic bag and some gloves?

22. Where do you keep your BBQ tongs?

23. Ouch, I pushed so hard my eye popped out!

103 Things To Say When You Leave The Bathroom

24. You're gonna wanna wash the windows in there...

25. You might as well just go ahead and repaint.

26. I would have been back sooner, but I had to fight that thing into submission!

103 Things To Say When You Leave The Bathroom

27. Enough roughage! I just pooped a fence post!

103 Things To Say When You Leave The Bathroom

28. Quick! Does anyone have a camera?

29. Now *there's* something you don't see everyday...

30. I don't even *remember* eating half of that stuff.

31. Did your toilet used to flush?

103 Things To Say When You Leave The Bathroom

32. I'm sorry if you heard me crying.

103 Things To Say When You Leave The Bathroom

33. So what *is* the deal with corn? I mean really!

103 Things To Say When You Leave The Bathroom

34. Just stocked the pond with brown trout!

35. Hey! I found the missing chess piece!

103 Things To Say When You Leave The Bathroom

36. Dude, I just *El Nino'd* in your *El Bano*.

37. Yeah...so you're going to need a new toilet seat!

103 Things To Say When You Leave The Bathroom

38. I left a gift in there for the next guy.

103 Things To Say When You Leave The Bathroom

39. I felt like it was my own...I couldn't bear to flush it.

103 Things To Say When You Leave The Bathroom

40. I have to repent for what just happened in your bathroom.

103 Things To Say When You Leave The Bathroom

41. Don't be surprised if the fire department stops by.

42. Does anyone know anything about hernias?

103 Things To Say When You Leave The Bathroom

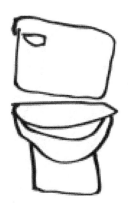

43. Holy Crap! I think I just pooped a pineapple!

103 Things To Say When You Leave The Bathroom

44. I just launched an urban assault on your house.

103 Things To Say When You Leave The Bathroom

45. Wow, I feel like I owe you money.

103 Things To Say When You Leave The Bathroom

46. I just dropped the kids off at the pool, and man did they put up a stink!

103 Things To Say When You Leave The Bathroom

47. I think I heard your toilet choke.

103 Things To Say When You Leave The Bathroom

48. The tooth fairy I am not, but I did leave you a gift.

103 Things To Say When You Leave The Bathroom

49. I just lost 10 pounds...the hard way.

50. Is there still skin on the back of my neck?

103 Things To Say When You Leave The Bathroom

51. I think I pushed your bathroom to a "code yellow."

52. Wow! Is anyone else seeing spots?

103 Things To Say When You Leave The Bathroom

53. Sorry about all the stomping.

103 Things To Say When You Leave The Bathroom

54. Next time I'll just go in the yard with your dog.

103 Things To Say When You Leave The Bathroom

55. Did my hair changed color in there?

56. Hey, I stripped the paint in there for ya!

103 Things To Say When You Leave The Bathroom

57. I was actually afraid to light the match.

58. Whoa, that thing swam two victory laps!

59. I may have just died and came back to life.

103 Things To Say When You Leave The Bathroom

60. You'd think that porcelain would be more durable...

103 Things To Say When You Leave The Bathroom

61. Well, *that* took five years off my life.

62. I should start taking a canary in there with me.

63. I definitely have a medical issue.

103 Things To Say When You Leave The Bathroom

64. I just did a number *three!*

103 Things To Say When You Leave The Bathroom

65. You may need to use gasoline on that stain.

103 Things To Say When You Leave The Bathroom

66. Man! Talk about your shock and awe!

103 Things To Say When You Leave The Bathroom

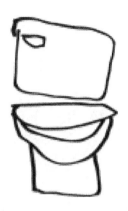

67. Can you boil some water? I need to wash
my hands.

103 Things To Say When You Leave The Bathroom

68. Careful with any open flames.

103 Things To Say When You Leave The Bathroom

69. If *that* wasn't against the law, it should be!

103 Things To Say When You Leave The Bathroom

70. Molly...I'm gonna need 16 more candles!

71. Do you guys have a mop...and a shovel?

103 Things To Say When You Leave The Bathroom

72. FIVE! That's a new flush record, baby!

103 Things To Say When You Leave The Bathroom

73. Does anyone have a change of clothes?

74. I just lowered the value of your house.

103 Things To Say When You Leave The Bathroom

75. There was something dead in there... but don't worry, I flushed it.

76. Whoa, I just pumped a grumpy!

103 Things To Say When You Leave The Bathroom

77. Now *that* was a royal flush!

103 Things To Say When You Leave The Bathroom

78. If your toilet was alive, it just died.

103 Things To Say When You Leave The Bathroom

79. Can we back a tow truck up to your bathroom?

103 Things To Say When You Leave The Bathroom

80. You should probably move that bird feeder away
from the bathroom window.

103 Things To Say When You Leave The Bathroom

81. I'm one step closer to the log cabin of my dreams!

103 Things To Say When You Leave The Bathroom

82. I actually got two inches of lift!

103 Things To Say When You Leave The Bathroom

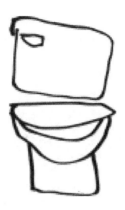

83. That's the last time I eat the gristle!

84. The stink actually took physical form and punched
me in the face!

85. I found the WOMD everyone's looking for.

103 Things To Say When You Leave The Bathroom

86. Whoa, that's the first time I've heard my butt scream...

103 Things To Say When You Leave The Bathroom

87. I actually made it rain in there.

103 Things To Say When You Leave The Bathroom

88. Anyone know what a radiation burn looks like?

103 Things To Say When You Leave The Bathroom

89. OK, first the good news...I can still walk...

90. I just discovered the cure for unwanted hair...

103 Things To Say When You Leave The Bathroom

91. First, I just want you all to know how much I appreciate you...

92. Wow, *that'll* put life into perspective!

103 Things To Say When You Leave The Bathroom

93. It's a good thing I had my gun with me, or it would
be something else standing here...

103 Things To Say When You Leave The Bathroom

94. Can someone find my wife and tell her that we
have a *Code 7*? I repeat a *Code 7*.

103 Things To Say When You Leave The Bathroom

95. Does anyone have a tic-tac for the toilet?

96. The candles were a good idea, but they really stood no chance.

103 Things To Say When You Leave The Bathroom

97. Whoa, that was the ugliest tadpole ever!

103 Things To Say When You Leave The Bathroom

100. I don't know what the weather is like out here, but in there...it's *musty*.

103 Things To Say When You Leave The Bathroom

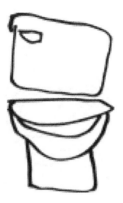

101.   I may have just discovered natural Novocain.

103 Things To Say When You Leave The Bathroom

102. Some ice water and a turkey baster, please?

103 Things To Say When You Leave The Bathroom

103. My life just flashed before my eye's. I just want to
tell you all how much I love you.

103 Things To Say When You Leave The Bathroom

Quick Order Form

Email orders: orders@elkmountainbooks.com
Postal orders: ElkMountainBooks, PO Box 21, Wilsonville, OR 97070, USA.
Telephone: 503-816-5937

Please send the following Books. I understand that I may return any of them for a full refund – for any reason – no questions asked.

___ Potty Talk @ $6.95ea   Total: _____

Name: _____   Address: _____

City: _____   State: _____   Zip: _____

Shipping:
Please add $2.50 (US) for the first book, and $1.00 (US) for each additional book. Credit card payments may be sent to: orders@perryperkinsbooks.com *via* www.paypal.com

See: http://www.perryperkinsbooks.com

103 Things To Say When You Leave The Bathroom

103 Things To Say When You Leave The Bathroom

Quick Order Form

Email orders: orders@elkmountainbooks.com
Online orders: www.elkmountainbooks.com
Postal orders: ElkMountainBooks, PO Box 21, Wilsonville, OR 97070, USA.
Telephone: 503-816-5937

Please send the following Books. I understand that I may return any of them for a full refund –
for any reason – no questions asked.

____ Potty Talk @ $6.95ea   Total: _____

Name: _____

Address: _____

City: _____ State: _____ Zip: _____

Shipping:
Please add $2.50 (US) for the first book, and $1.00 (US) for each additional book. Credit card
payments may be sent to: orders@perryperkinsbooks.com *via* www.paypal.com

See: http://www.elkmountainbooks.com

103 Things To Say When You Leave The Bathroom

Made in the USA
Las Vegas, NV
14 December 2022

62625712R00063